barbecue

A selection of delicious sizzlers

p

This is a Parragon Book
This edition published in 2006

Parragon
Queen Street House
4 Queen Street
Bath BA1 1HE

ISBN: 978-1-4054-8759-7

Printed in China

Cover by Talking Design

This book uses metric and imperial measurements. Follow the same units of measurement throughout; do not mix metric and imperial.

All spoon measurements are level, unless otherwise stated: teaspoons are assumed to be 5ml and tablespoons are assumed to be 15ml.

Unless otherwise stated, milk is assumed to be whole, eggs and individual fruits such as bananas are medium, and pepper is freshly ground black pepper.

Recipes using raw or very lightly cooked eggs should be avoided by infants, the elderly, pregnant women, convalescents and anyone suffering from an illness. Pregnant and breast-feeding women are advised to avoid eating peanuts and peanut products.

contents

introduction

Just the scent of a barbecue can conjure up memories of lazy summer evenings. Delicious aromas wafting from a campfire in the countryside, on the beach or from your back garden, evoke scenes of leisurely meals with family and friends. Wherever you choose to have your barbecue the atmosphere is always relaxed and the usual pressures that accompany meal preparations when cooking for guests do not apply. Having a barbecue is quite simply one of the most informal and sociable ways of entertaining – just cooking outdoors on a sizzling barbecue is a fun way to cook fabulous food, providing the opportunity to mingle and enjoy the atmosphere with your guests whilst still cooking a delicious spread. Whether you are cooking a small weekend lunch for the family or throwing a summer party for 20 guests, a barbecue can provide plenty of variety and entertainment for everyone.

Although meat is the traditional staple of a barbecue, vegetarians can also enjoy a wide variety of barbecued dishes. This book features traditional barbecue dishes, as well as more exotic and unusual ones. You can begin by cooking simple foods, such as sausages, hamburgers and steaks, until you build up your confidence and become more familiar with your barbecue. When you feel that you are ready to try something more complicated, experiment with meats, vegetables, marinades and a range of different dishes.

Planning and preparation

The key to a successful barbecue is planning.

• Arrange all the food to be barbecued on trays or large platters and have clean trays and platters ready to carry the food once it is cooked. Remember to provide tomato ketchup, mustard, barbecue relishes and any other sauces your guests would enjoy, together with lots of burger buns and a selection of breads.

• Food to be marinated should ideally be prepared the day before, so that the flavours can be fully absorbed. The exception is a citrus marinade with fish, as the juice begins to 'cook' the fish after about 1 hour.

• If using wooden skewers, remember to soak them in water for at least 30 minutes before skewering ingredients. This will prevent the skewers burning.

• Light your barbecue at least one hour before you begin cooking so that it is really hot, and follow the fuel manufacturer's instructions exactly for safety and best results.

• Do not overcrowd the metal rack, or food will not cook evenly and right through to the centre.

- Keep similar foods together while cooking and do not mix meat, fish and vegetables.
- Assemble and dress salads just before serving for maximum freshness and to prevent the leaves going soggy.

What to serve

Try to plan the menu so that there is something for everyone. There may be vegetarian guests, fussy children or meat-eaters not keen on salads, so offer a range of dishes. Remember to provide bread or potatoes to accompany the meat, fish and vegetable dishes. Foil-wrapped baked potatoes cooked in the coals of the barbecue are the easiest. Preheat the oven to 200°C/400°F/Gas Mark 6 and cook the potatoes for 30 minutes, before transferring to the barbecue, as they can take a long time to cook.

Offer a choice of drinks, alcoholic and non-alcoholic. Whilst fruit punch with little or no alcohol is usually popular, mineral water, fruit juice and iced tea will all be very welcome. Desserts can also be kept simple. Barbecue fruit in foil parcels or serve fresh fruit and a generous, varied cheeseboard. However, don't be afraid to try something special: have a look at the section on

desserts and home-made beverages (pages 154-175) for delicious dishes that will really add the finishing touch to your barbecue.

Hints and tips

- It helps to know roughly how many people are coming. However, if you are unsure of exactly how many guests to expect, make sure that you have a good supply of basics, such as burgers, so everyone has enough to eat.
- You can make dishes for your barbecue well in advance. Make and freeze kebabs and burgers, although fish kebabs tend not to freeze well. Remove from the freezer 24 hours in advance and thaw in the refrigerator.
- When you have lit the barbecue, you can begin to bring the meat outside. Brush the grill rack with a little sunflower oil to stop food sticking, being careful not to drip too much oil on to the hot coals.
- Try to cook the same types of food at the same time to avoid contamination. The coals should cover an area wider than that of the food, so even the edges of the grill rack should be quite hot. Use the edges to cook foods that require a lower heat to save having to let the barbecue cool down.
- Even if rain interrupts your barbecue, the party can continue – just pull the lid over the barbecue and open its air vents to continue cooking. Alternatively, take the prepared food inside and carry on cooking under the grill in your kitchen. When the rain stops, the party can return to the garden!

Types of fuel

There are different types of fuel and you should consider which type you would prefer to use before buying your barbecue.

Lumpwood charcoal

• Easy to ignite, but will burn quite quickly. It is relatively inexpensive.

Charcoal briquettes

• Can take a while to ignite, however they burn for a long time with little smell or smoke. They are ideal for a small garden where the barbecue is near windows and other people's houses.

Self-igniting charcoal

• Lumpwood charcoal or briquettes that have been coated with a flammable chemical. You must wait until the chemical has burnt off before adding food to the barbecue.

Wood chips and herbs can be added to the fire, but not used as a main fuel. Sprigs of rosemary, thyme and sage scattered over the hot coals or wood underneath the food will give off a delicious aroma.

Types of barbecue

There are many different types of barbecue available. Think carefully about what you want to get out of your barbecue before buying. Bear in mind how many people you are likely to be cooking for and how large your garden is. Will the smoke annoy your neighbours? Should you consider a built-in brick barbecue? What type of fuel would you prefer to use?

Disposable barbecues

Usually little more than foil trays with a rack resting near the top, disposable barbecues are adequate for a small picnic or lunch. They are inexpensive but can only be used once.

Portable barbecues

These vary in size and price and are a popular choice. They are light to carry and fold away to fit into a car boot. These are ideal for a larger picnic where you will not have to walk too far. They are easy to clean.

Brazier barbecues

Another popular choice. Although you could not transport a brazier barbecue to a picnic, it can easily be moved into a shed for storage. If your garden is windy, a brazier may not be the best choice since these are open barbecues, although many do have a hood to offer some protection.

Kettle-grill barbecues

Very versatile and efficient. The large lid offers protection from the wind and can rescue a barbecue party if the weather is unfavourable. Joints of meat or whole chickens can be cooked on this type of barbecue. Meat cooks evenly and it is easy to control the heat using the air vents.

Gas and electric barbecues

These warm up very quickly but tend to be expensive. They are easy to operate, although they do not produce the traditional smoky flavour of grilling over charcoal.

Permanent barbecues

These would be an excellent choice if you plan to barbecue frequently. They can be built to the right size for your family and do not have to be expensive. Choose the best site for your barbecue: it should be a little distance from your neighbours, but as close to the kitchen as possible.

Safety

• Barbecuing is a safe way of cooking as long as you are sensible. Try not to be over-ambitious if you have not used a barbecue before and always err on the side of caution.

• Ensure that your barbecue is stable and on a flat surface before you light it. Once it is lit, do not move it.

• Keep the barbecue away from trees and shrubs. Note which way the wind is blowing before lighting the barbecue.

• Never add any flammable liquids to try to speed up the ignition of the barbecue. Only ever use fuels designed for the purpose, such as firelighter cubes and liquid.

• Always have a bucket of water nearby in case the fire gets out of control. If your barbecue has a lid, this will also help to control the flames.

• Trim excess fats from meats and shake or scrape off any excess marinade before adding to the barbecue. Fat dripping from meat will make the coals flare up and can cause flames to get out of control.

• To avoid salmonella, listeria and food poisoning, always make sure that meat is cooked through. Pay attention in particular to chicken, turkey and pork. The cooked meat should have no pink flesh and the juices should run clear (not pink) when the meat is pierced through the thickest part with a skewer or the point of a sharp knife.

• Keep salads and cooked foods away from raw meat and wash your hands carefully after handling raw meat. Use different chopping boards, serving plates and utensils for raw meats.

• Keep pets and children away from the barbecue. Always have another adult nearby to supervise the children when you are cooking.

• Use utensils with long handles and make sure you have a range of tools handy so you do not leave the barbecue unattended. Oven gloves are useful, as the barbecue may become very hot after a while. Plastic utensils should be avoided, as the intense heat from the barbecue can melt them. Metal utensils are best but remember that they can get very hot.

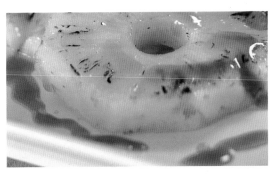

marvellous **meat**

Meat is the traditional barbecue staple but you do not need to limit yourself to ready-made burgers and sausages. Delight your guests by offering a range of different meats and flavours. Kebabs using a variety of lean cuts are easy to prepare, whilst marinades lend a whole new dimension of flavour to simple steaks and chops and make the meat wonderfully tender.

These spicy Indonesian kebabs are served with a delicious chilli-flavoured dipping sauce.

indonesian beef kebabs

1 tsp coriander seeds
$1/2$ tsp cumin seeds
450 g/1 lb rump steak
cut into strips
1 onion
2 garlic cloves
1 tbsp muscovado sugar
1 tbsp dark soy sauce
4 tbsp lemon juice
salt

SAUCE
1 fresh red chilli
4 tbsp dark soy sauce
2 garlic cloves, finely chopped
4 tsp lemon juice
2 tbsp hot water

SERVES 4

To make the sauce, using a sharp knife, deseed the chilli and finely chop. Place in a small bowl with all the other sauce ingredients and mix together. Cover with clingfilm and leave to stand until required.

Dry-fry the coriander and cumin seeds in a frying pan for 1 minute, or until they give off their aroma and begin to pop. Remove from the heat and grind in a mortar with a pestle. Place the steak in a shallow, non-metallic dish and add the ground spices, stirring to coat. Put the onion, garlic, sugar, soy sauce and lemon juice into a food processor and process to a paste. Season to taste with salt and spoon the mixture over the steak, turning to coat. Cover with clingfilm and leave to marinate in the refrigerator for 2 hours.

Preheat the barbecue. Drain the steak, reserving the marinade, and thread it on to several presoaked wooden or metal skewers. Cook over hot coals, turning and basting frequently with the reserved marinade, for 5–8 minutes, until thoroughly cooked. Transfer to a large serving plate and serve with the sauce for dipping.

These traditional Turkish kebabs make an excellent addition to a barbecue.

turkish kebabs

500 g/1 lb 2 oz boned
shoulder of lamb, cut into
2.5-cm/1-inch cubes
1 tbsp olive oil
2 tbsp dry white wine
2 tbsp finely chopped fresh mint
4 garlic cloves, finely chopped
2 tsp grated orange rind
1 tbsp paprika
1 tsp sugar
salt and pepper

TAHINI CREAM
225 g/8 oz tahini paste
2 garlic cloves, finely chopped
2 tbsp extra-virgin olive oil
2 tbsp lemon juice
125 ml/4 fl oz water

SERVES 4

Place the lamb cubes in a large, shallow, non-metallic dish. Mix the olive oil, wine, mint, garlic, orange rind, paprika and sugar together in a jug and season to taste with salt and pepper. Pour the mixture over the lamb, turning to coat, then cover with clingfilm and leave to marinate in the refrigerator for 2 hours, turning occasionally.

Preheat the barbecue. To make the tahini cream, put the tahini paste, garlic, oil and lemon juice into a food processor and process briefly to mix. With the motor still running, gradually add the water through the feeder tube until smooth. Transfer to a bowl, cover with clingfilm and leave to chill in the refrigerator until required.

Drain the lamb, reserving the marinade, and thread it on to several long metal skewers. Cook over medium hot coals, turning and brushing frequently with the reserved marinade, for 10–15 minutes. Serve with the tahini cream.

These kebabs have a delicious, slightly sweet flavour that is popular with children.

pork and sage kebabs

450 g/1 lb pork mince
25 g/1 oz fresh breadcrumbs
1 small onion, chopped
very finely
1 tbsp fresh sage, chopped
2 tbsp apple sauce
1/4 tsp ground nutmeg
salt and pepper

BASTE
3 tbsp olive oil
1 tbsp lemon juice

TO SERVE
6 small pitta breads
mixed salad leaves
6 tbsp thick, natural yogurt

MAKES 12

Place the mince in a mixing bowl together with the breadcrumbs, onion, sage, apple sauce, nutmeg and salt and pepper to taste. Mix until the ingredients are well combined.

Using your hands, shape the mixture into small balls, about the size of large marbles, and leave to chill in the refrigerator for at least 30 minutes.

Meanwhile, soak 12 small wooden skewers in cold water for at least 30 minutes. Thread the meatballs on to the skewers.

To make the baste, mix together the oil and lemon juice in a small bowl, whisking with a fork until it is well blended.

Barbecue the kebabs over hot coals for 8–10 minutes, turning and basting frequently with the lemon and oil mixture, until the meat is golden and cooked through.

Line the pitta breads with the salad leaves and spoon over some of the yogurt. Serve with the kebabs.

A subtle combination of flavours makes this a stylish dish for a barbecue.

curried lamb skewers

MARINADE
2 tsp vegetable oil
1 tsp curry powder
1 tsp garam masala
2 tsp granulated sugar
200 ml/7fl oz natural yogurt

SKEWERS
400 g/14 oz boneless lamb, cubed
140 g/5 oz dried apricot halves
1 red or green pepper, deseeded and cut into small chunks
2 courgettes, cubed
16 baby onions

TO SERVE
freshly steamed or boiled rice
crisp green salad leaves

TO GARNISH
fresh coriander leaves

SERVES 4

Put the oil, spices, sugar and yogurt into a large bowl and mix until well combined.

Thread the lamb onto 8 skewers, alternating it with the apricot halves, red or green pepper, courgettes and baby onions. When the skewers are full (leave a small space at either end), transfer them to the bowl and turn them in the yogurt mixture until they are well coated. Cover with clingfilm and place in the refrigerator to marinate for at least 8 hours or overnight.

When the skewers are thoroughly marinated, lift them out and barbecue them over hot coals, turning them frequently, for 15 minutes, or until the meat is cooked right through. Serve at once with freshly cooked rice or a crisp green salad, garnished with fresh coriander leaves.

A spicy, flavoursome treat for a special barbecue.

thai-spiced beef and pepper kebabs

MARINADE
2 tbsp sherry
2 tbsp rice wine
75 ml/2^1/$_2$ fl oz soy sauce
75 ml/2^1/$_2$ fl oz hoisin sauce
3 cloves garlic, finely chopped
1 red chilli, deseeded and
finely chopped
1^1/$_2$ tbsp grated fresh root
ginger
3 spring onions, trimmed and
finely chopped
salt and pepper

KEBABS
1 kg/2 lb 4 oz rump or sirloin
steak, cubed
2 large red peppers, deseeded
and cut into small chunks

TO SERVE
green and red lettuce leaves

SERVES 4

Put the sherry, rice wine, soy sauce, hoisin sauce, garlic, chilli, ginger and spring onions into a large bowl and mix until well combined. Season to taste.

Thread the meat onto 8 skewers, alternating it with chunks of red pepper. When the skewers are full (leave a small space at either end), transfer them to the bowl and turn them in the soy sauce mixture until they are well coated. Cover with clingfilm and place in the refrigerator to marinate for at least 2^1/$_2$ hours or overnight.

When the skewers are thoroughly marinated, lift them out and barbecue them over hot coals, turning them frequently, for 10–15 minutes, or until the meat is cooked right through. Serve at once on a bed of green and red lettuce leaves.

A tasty traditional barbecue dish – with an extra spiciness.

beefburgers with chilli and basil

650 g/1 lb 7 oz minced beef
1 red pepper, deseeded and
finely chopped
1 garlic clove, finely chopped
2 small red chillies, deseeded
and finely chopped
1 tbsp chopped fresh basil
1/2 tsp powdered cumin
salt and pepper

TO SERVE
sprigs of fresh basil
4 hamburger buns

SERVES 4

Put the minced beef, red pepper, garlic, chillies, chopped basil and cumin into a bowl and mix until well combined. Season with salt and pepper.

Using your hands, form the mixture into burger shapes. Barbecue the burgers over hot coals for 5–8 minutes on each side, or until cooked right through. Garnish with sprigs of basil and serve in hamburger buns.

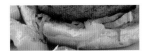

Lamb and fresh mint are a classic partnership.

minty lamb burgers

1 red pepper, deseeded
and cut into quarters
1 yellow pepper, deseeded
and cut into quarters
1 red onion, cut into
thick wedges
1 baby aubergine (115 g/4 oz),
cut into wedges
2 tbsp olive oil
450 g/1 lb fresh lamb mince
2 tbsp freshly grated
Parmesan cheese
1 tbsp chopped fresh mint
salt and pepper

MINTY MUSTARD MAYO
4 tbsp mayonnaise
1 tsp Dijon mustard
1 tbsp chopped fresh mint

TO SERVE
shredded lettuce
4 hamburger buns

SERVES 4–5

Preheat the grill to medium. Place the peppers, onion and aubergine on a foil-lined grill rack, brush the aubergine with 1 tablespoon of the oil and cook under the hot grill for 10–12 minutes, or until charred. Remove from the grill, leave to cool, then peel the peppers. Place all the vegetables in a food processor and, using the pulse button, chop.

Add the lamb mince, Parmesan cheese, chopped mint and salt and pepper to the food processor and blend until the mixture comes together. Scrape on to a board and shape into 4–6 equal-sized burgers. Cover and leave to chill for at least 30 minutes.

To make the minty mustard mayo, blend the mayonnaise with the Dijon mustard and chopped fresh mint. Refrigerate until required.

Preheat the barbecue. Lightly brush the burgers with the remaining oil, then cook over hot coals for 3–4 minutes on each side or until cooked to personal preference.

Arrange the shredded lettuce on the bases of the hamburger buns. Add the burgers and top with a spoonful of the minty mustard mayonnaise. Serve.

The large pieces of orange peel in the marmalade add extra texture to this burger.

pork burgers with tangy orange marinade

450 g/1 lb pork fillet, cut into
small pieces
3 tbsp Seville orange
marmalade
2 tbsp orange juice
1 tbsp balsamic vinegar
225 g/8 oz parsnips,
cut into chunks
1 tbsp finely grated orange rind
2 garlic cloves, crushed
6 spring onions, finely chopped
1 courgette (175 g/6 oz), grated
salt and pepper
1 tbsp sunflower oil

TO SERVE
salad leaves
4 hamburger buns

SERVES 4–6

Place the pork in a shallow dish. Place the marmalade, orange juice and vinegar in a small saucepan and heat, stirring, until the marmalade has melted. Pour the marinade over the pork. Cover and leave for at least 30 minutes, or longer if time permits. Remove the pork, reserving the marinade. Mince the pork into a large bowl.

Meanwhile, cook the parsnips in a saucepan of boiling water for 15–20 minutes, or until cooked. Drain, then mash and add to the pork. Stir in the orange rind, garlic, spring onions, courgette and salt and pepper to taste. Mix together, then shape into 4–6 equal-sized burgers. Cover and leave to chill for at least 30 minutes.

Preheat the barbecue. Lightly brush each burger with a little oil and then add them to the barbecue grill, cooking over medium hot coals for 4–6 minutes on each side or until thoroughly cooked. Boil the reserved marinade for 3 minutes, then pour into a small jug or bowl.

Arrange the salad leaves on the bases of the hamburger buns. Add the burgers and pour over a little of the marinade. Serve.

For an extra spicy kick, add a spoonful of mustard to the cooked burger.

the ultimate cheeseburger

450 g/1 lb best steak mince
4 onions
2–4 garlic cloves, crushed
2–3 tsp grated fresh horseradish
or 1–1¹/₂ tbsp creamed
horseradish
pepper
8 lean back bacon rashers
2 tbsp sunflower oil

TO SERVE
shredded lettuce
4 hamburger buns
4 slices cheese

SERVES 4

Place the steak mince in a large bowl. Finely grate 1 of the onions and add to the steak mince in the bowl.

Add the garlic, horseradish and pepper to the steak mixture in the bowl. Mix together, then shape into 4 equal-sized burgers. Wrap each burger in 2 rashers of bacon, then cover and leave to chill for 30 minutes. Slice the remaining onions. Heat the oil in a frying pan. Slice the remaining onions finely, add to the frying pan and cook over a medium heat for 8–10 minutes, stirring frequently, until the onions are golden brown. Drain on kitchen paper and keep warm.

Preheat the barbecue. Cook the burgers over hot coals for 3–5 minutes on each side or until cooked to personal preference.

Arrange the shredded lettuce on the bases of the hamburger buns. Add the burgers, some of the fried onion and a slice of cheese. If desired, place under a grill for 1–2 minutes to melt the cheese. Serve.

Home-made sausages are made even more tempting with these tasty ingredients.

barbecued pork sausages with thyme

1 garlic clove, finely chopped
1 onion, grated
1 small red chilli, deseeded and
finely chopped
450 g/1 lb lean minced pork
50 g/1³/₄ oz almonds, toasted
and ground
50 g/1³/₄ oz fresh breadcrumbs
1 tbsp finely chopped
fresh thyme
salt and pepper
flour, for dusting
vegetable oil, for brushing

TO SERVE
fresh finger rolls
slices of onion, lightly cooked
tomato ketchup and/or mustard

SERVES 4

Put the garlic, onion, chilli, pork, almonds, breadcrumbs and fresh thyme into a large bowl. Season well with salt and pepper and mix until well combined.

Using your hands, form the mixture into sausage shapes. Roll each sausage in a little flour, then transfer to a bowl, cover with clingfilm and refrigerate for 45 minutes.

Brush a piece of aluminium foil with oil, then put the sausages on the foil and brush them with a little more vegetable oil. Transfer the sausages and foil to the barbecue.

Barbecue over hot coals, turning the sausages frequently, for about 15 minutes, or until cooked right through. Serve with finger rolls, cooked sliced onion and tomato ketchup and/or mustard.

 Succulent steaks are made extra special with a tangy blue cheese topping.

steak with blue cheese topping

MARINADE
150 ml/5 fl oz red wine
1 tbsp red wine vinegar
1 tbsp olive oil
1 garlic clove, finely chopped
1 bay leaf, crumbled
1 tbsp wholegrain mustard
4 rump or sirloin steaks, about
175 g/6 oz each
55 g/2 oz blue cheese,
such as Gorgonzola
55 g/2 oz fresh white
breadcrumbs
2 tbsp chopped fresh parsley

TO GARNISH
a small salad

SERVES 4

Mix together the red wine, vinegar, olive oil, garlic, bay leaf and mustard in a shallow dish. Add the steaks, turning to coat, then cover and leave in a cool place to marinate for 4 hours.

Meanwhile, mix together the blue cheese, breadcrumbs and parsley in a small bowl. Cover and store in the refrigerator until required.

Drain the steaks. Cook on a preheated barbecue for 4–6 minutes on each side or until cooked to personal preference. Spoon the cheese topping onto the steaks, pressing it down with the back of a spoon. Serve at once, garnished with a small salad.

These chops will only need marinating for a short time, as the marinade is quite strongly flavoured.

sozzled lamb chops

8 lamb loin chops

MARINADE
2 tbsp extra-virgin olive oil
2 tbsp Worcestershire sauce
2 tbsp lemon juice
2 tbsp dry gin
1 garlic clove, finely chopped
salt and pepper

MUSTARD BUTTER
55 g/2 oz unsalted butter, softened
$1^1/_2$ tsp tarragon mustard
1 tbsp chopped fresh parsley
dash of lemon juice

TO GARNISH
fresh parsley sprigs

TO SERVE
salad

SERVES 4

Preheat the barbecue. Place the lamb chops in a large, shallow, non-metallic dish. Mix all the ingredients for the marinade together in a jug, seasoning to taste with salt and pepper. Pour the mixture over the chops and then turn them until they are thoroughly coated. Cover with clingfilm and leave to marinate for 5 minutes.

To make the mustard butter, mix all the ingredients together in a small bowl, beating with a fork until well blended. Cover with clingfilm and leave to chill in the refrigerator until required.

Drain the chops, reserving the marinade. Cook over medium hot coals, brushing frequently with the reserved marinade, for 5 minutes on each side. Transfer to serving plates, top with the mustard butter and garnish with parsley sprigs. Serve immediately with salad.

These rosemary-flavoured lamb chops are a popular choice for a weekend barbecue.

lamb cutlets with rosemary

8 lamb cutlets
5 tbsp olive oil
2 tbsp lemon juice
1 garlic clove, crushed
$1/2$ tsp lemon pepper
salt
8 fresh rosemary sprigs

SALAD
4 tomatoes, sliced
4 spring onions,
diagonally sliced

DRESSING
2 tbsp olive oil
1 tbsp lemon juice
1 garlic clove, chopped
$1/4$ tsp finely chopped
fresh rosemary

SERVES 4

Preheat the barbecue. Trim the lamb by cutting away the flesh to expose the tips of the bones.

Place the oil, lemon juice, garlic, lemon pepper and salt in a shallow non-metallic dish and whisk with a fork to combine.

Lay the rosemary sprigs in the dish and place the lamb on top. Cover and leave to marinate for at least 1 hour, turning the lamb cutlets once.

Remove the chops from the marinade and wrap foil around the exposed bones to stop them from burning.

Place the rosemary sprigs on the rack and place the lamb on top. Barbecue over hot coals for 10–15 minutes, turning once.

Meanwhile, make the salad and dressing. Arrange the tomatoes on a serving dish and sprinkle the spring onions on top. Place all the ingredients for the dressing in a screw-top jar, shake well and pour over the salad. Serve with the barbecued lamb cutlets.

These tasty pork chops are cooked with a mouthwatering honey glaze.

honey-glazed pork chops

4 lean pork loin chops
salt and pepper
4 tbsp clear honey
1 tbsp dry sherry
4 tbsp orange juice
2 tbsp olive oil
2.5-cm/1-inch piece fresh root
ginger, grated
sunflower oil, for oiling

SERVES 4

Preheat the barbecue. Season the pork chops with salt and pepper to taste. Reserve while you make the glaze.

To make the glaze, place the honey, sherry, orange juice, olive oil and ginger in a small saucepan and heat gently, stirring constantly, until well blended.

Cook the pork chops on an oiled rack over hot coals for 5 minutes on each side.

Brush the chops with the glaze and barbecue for a further 2–4 minutes on each side, basting frequently with the glaze.

Transfer the pork chops to warmed serving plates and serve hot.

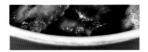

These succulent pork spare ribs are deliciously tender and packed full of spicy flavours.

hot and spicy ribs

1 onion, chopped
2 garlic cloves, chopped
2.5-cm/1-inch piece fresh root ginger, sliced
1 fresh red chilli, deseeded and chopped
5 tbsp dark soy sauce
3 tbsp lime juice
1 tbsp palm or muscovado sugar
2 tbsp groundnut oil
salt and pepper
1 kg/2 lb 4 oz pork spare ribs, separated

SERVES 4

Preheat the barbecue. Put the onion, garlic, ginger, chilli and soy sauce into a food processor and process to a paste. Transfer to a jug and stir in the lime juice, sugar and oil and season to taste with salt and pepper.

Place the spare ribs in a preheated wok or large, heavy-based saucepan and pour in the soy sauce mixture. Place on the hob and bring to the boil, then simmer over a low heat, stirring frequently, for 30 minutes. If the mixture appears to be drying out, add a little water.

Remove the spare ribs, reserving the sauce. Cook the ribs over medium hot coals, turning and basting frequently with the sauce, for 20–30 minutes. Transfer to a large serving plate and serve immediately.

The wonderful flavours in the marinade make these ribs a tasty treat.

chinese ribs

1 kg/2 lb 4 oz pork spare ribs, separated
4 tbsp dark soy sauce
3 tbsp muscovado sugar
1 tbsp groundnut or sunflower oil
2 garlic cloves, finely chopped
2 tsp Chinese five-spice powder
1-cm/½-inch piece fresh root ginger, grated

TO GARNISH
shredded spring onions

SERVES 4

Place the spare ribs in a large, shallow, non-metallic dish. Mix the soy sauce, sugar, oil, garlic, Chinese five-spice powder and ginger together in a bowl. Pour the mixture over the ribs and turn until the ribs are thoroughly coated in the marinade.

Cover the dish with clingfilm and leave to marinate in the refrigerator for at least 6 hours.

Preheat the barbecue. Drain the ribs, reserving the marinade. Cook over medium hot coals, turning and brushing frequently with the reserved marinade, for 30–40 minutes. Transfer to a large serving dish, garnish with the shredded spring onions and serve immediately.

perfect **poultry**

Chicken and other poultry are always a popular choice for a barbecue and this chapter explores their amazing versatility. There are family favourites using inexpensive chicken drumsticks and portions as well as a selection of more exotic dishes for when you want to impress. Whether you like your food hot and spicy, subtle and aromatic or fruity and refreshing, you are sure to find a dish to set your taste buds tingling.

 These lovely, fresh-tasting chicken kebabs are marinated in a zingy mixture of citrus juice and rind.

zesty **kebabs**

4 skinless, boneless
chicken breasts, about
175 g/6 oz each
finely grated rind and
juice of 1/2 lemon
finely grated rind and
juice of 1/2 orange
2 tbsp clear honey
2 tbsp olive oil
2 tbsp chopped fresh mint
1/4 tsp ground coriander
salt and pepper

TO GARNISH
fresh mint sprigs
citrus zest

SERVES 4

Using a sharp knife, cut the chicken into 2.5-cm/1-inch cubes, then place them in a large glass bowl. Place the lemon and orange rind, the lemon and orange juice, the honey, oil, mint and ground coriander in a jug and mix together. Season to taste with salt and pepper. Pour the marinade over the chicken cubes and toss until they are thoroughly coated. Cover with clingfilm and leave to marinate in the refrigerator for up to 8 hours.

Preheat the barbecue. Drain the chicken cubes, reserving the marinade. Thread the chicken on to several long metal skewers.

Cook the skewers over medium hot coals, turning and brushing frequently with the reserved marinade, for 6–10 minutes, or until thoroughly cooked. Transfer to a large serving plate, garnish with fresh mint sprigs and citrus zest and serve immediately.

Lime juice combined with warm spices makes this a dish to remember.

chicken satay skewers with lime

MARINADE
100 ml/3^1/$_2$ fl oz soy sauce
100 ml/3^1/$_2$ fl oz lime juice
2 tbsp smooth peanut butter
2 tbsp garam masala
1 tbsp brown sugar
2 garlic cloves, finely chopped
1 small red chilli, deseeded and finely chopped
pepper

SKEWERS
6 skinless, boneless chicken breasts, cubed

TO SERVE
freshly steamed or boiled rice or crisp green salad leaves

TO GARNISH
fresh coriander leaves, shredded
wedges of lime

SERVES 4

Put the soy sauce, lime juice, peanut butter, garam masala, sugar, garlic and chilli into a large bowl and mix until well combined. Season with plenty of pepper.

Thread the chicken cubes onto skewers (leave a small space at either end). Transfer them to the bowl and turn them in the peanut butter mixture until they are well coated. Cover with clingfilm and place in the refrigerator to marinate for at least 2^1/$_2$ hours.

When the skewers are thoroughly marinated, lift them out and barbecue them over hot coals for 15 minutes, or until cooked right through, turning them frequently and basting with the remaining marinade. Arrange the skewers on a bed of freshly cooked rice or crisp green salad leaves, garnish with coriander leaves and lime wedges and serve.

Full of Mediterranean flavours, these turkey kebabs taste fabulous.

turkey with coriander pesto

450 g/1 lb skinless, boneless turkey, cut into 5-cm/2-inch cubes
2 courgettes, thickly sliced
1 red and 1 yellow pepper, deseeded and cut into 5-cm/2-inch squares
8 cherry tomatoes
8 baby onions

MARINADE
6 tbsp olive oil
3 tbsp dry white wine
1 tsp green peppercorns, crushed
2 tbsp chopped fresh coriander
salt

CORIANDER PESTO
55 g/2 oz fresh coriander leaves
15 g/1/2 oz fresh parsley leaves
1 garlic clove
55 g/2 oz pine kernels
25 g/1 oz freshly grated Parmesan cheese
6 tbsp extra-virgin olive oil
juice of 1 lemon

SERVES 4

Place the turkey in a large glass bowl. To make the marinade, mix the olive oil, wine, peppercorns and coriander together in a jug and season to taste with salt. Pour the mixture over the turkey and turn until the turkey is thoroughly coated. Cover with clingfilm and leave to marinate in the refrigerator for 2 hours.

Preheat the barbecue. To make the pesto, put the coriander and parsley into a food processor and process until finely chopped. Add the garlic and pine kernels and pulse until chopped. Add the Parmesan cheese, oil and lemon juice and process briefly to mix. Transfer to a bowl, cover and leave to chill in the refrigerator until required.

Drain the turkey, reserving the marinade. Thread the turkey, courgette slices, pepper pieces, cherry tomatoes and onions alternately on to metal skewers. Cook over medium hot coals, turning and brushing frequently with the marinade, for 10 minutes. Serve immediately with the coriander pesto.

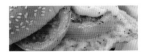

These deliciously tender, thin pieces of breaded chicken will be enjoyed by all.

the ultimate chicken burger

4 large chicken breast fillets, skinned
1 large egg white
1 tbsp cornflour
1 tbsp plain flour
1 egg, beaten
55 g/2 oz fresh white breadcrumbs
2 tbsp sunflower oil

TO SERVE
shredded lettuce
4 hamburger buns
2 beef tomatoes, sliced
mayonnaise

SERVES 4

Place the chicken breasts between 2 sheets of non-stick baking paper and flatten slightly using a meat mallet or a rolling pin. Beat the egg white and cornflour together, then brush over the chicken. Cover and leave to chill for 30 minutes, then coat in the flour.

Place the egg and breadcrumbs in 2 separate bowls and coat the burgers first in the egg, allowing any excess to drip back into the bowl, then in the breadcrumbs.

Preheat the barbecue. Lightly brush each burger with a little oil and then add them to the barbecue grill, cooking over medium hot coals for 6–8 minutes on each side, or until thoroughly cooked. If you are in doubt, it is worth cutting one of the burgers in half. If there is any sign of pinkness, cook for a little longer to get that nice barbecue taste.

Arrange the shredded lettuce on the bases of the hamburger buns. Add the burgers and top with the sliced tomatoes and a little mayonnaise. Serve.

The sweet-and-sour glaze gives the chicken a wonderful piquancy.

mustard and honey drumsticks

8 chicken drumsticks

GLAZE
125 ml/4 fl oz clear honey
4 tbsp Dijon mustard
4 tbsp wholegrain mustard
4 tbsp white wine vinegar
2 tbsp sunflower oil
salt and pepper

TO GARNISH
fresh parsley sprigs

TO SERVE
salad

SERVES 4

Using a sharp knife, make 2–3 diagonal slashes in the chicken drumsticks and place them in a large, non-metallic dish.

Mix all the ingredients for the glaze together in a jug and season to taste with salt and pepper. Pour the glaze over the drumsticks, turning until the drumsticks are well coated. Cover with clingfilm and leave to marinate in the refrigerator for at least 1 hour.

Preheat the barbecue. Drain the chicken drumsticks, reserving the marinade. Cook the chicken over medium hot coals, turning frequently and brushing with the reserved marinade, for 25–30 minutes, or until thoroughly cooked. Transfer to serving plates, garnish with fresh parsley sprigs and serve immediately with salad.

This is perhaps one of the best known Caribbean dishes. The 'jerk' in the name refers to the hot spicy coating.

jerk chicken

4 lean chicken portions
1 bunch spring onions, trimmed
1–2 Scotch Bonnet chillies, deseeded
1 garlic clove
5 cm/2 inch piece root ginger, peeled and roughly chopped
$1/2$ tsp dried thyme
$1/2$ tsp paprika
$1/4$ tsp ground allspice
pinch ground cinnamon
pinch ground cloves
4 tbsp white wine vinegar
3 tbsp light soy sauce
pepper

SERVES 4

Rinse the chicken portions and pat them dry on absorbent kitchen paper. Place them in a shallow dish.

Place the spring onions, chillies, garlic, ginger, thyme, paprika, allspice, cinnamon, cloves, wine vinegar, soy sauce and pepper to taste in a food processor and process until smooth.

Pour the spicy mixture over the chicken. Turn the chicken portions over so that they are well coated in the marinade.

Transfer the chicken portions to the refrigerator and leave to marinate for up to 24 hours.

Remove the chicken from the marinade and barbecue over medium hot coals for about 30 minutes, turning the chicken over and basting occasionally with any remaining marinade, until the chicken is browned and cooked through.

Transfer the chicken portions to individual serving plates and serve at once.

Chicken and corn are coated in an aromatic spice mix for a sizzling surprise.

cajun **chicken**

4 chicken drumsticks
4 chicken thighs
2 fresh corn cobs, husks and
silks removed
85 g/3 oz butter, melted

SPICE MIX
2 tsp onion powder
2 tsp paprika
1^1/$_2$ tsp salt
1 tsp garlic powder
1 tsp dried thyme
1 tsp cayenne pepper
1 tsp ground black pepper
^{1}/$_2$ tsp ground white pepper
^{1}/$_4$ tsp ground cumin

SERVES 4

Preheat the barbecue. Using a sharp knife, make 2–3 diagonal slashes in the chicken drumsticks and thighs, then place them in a large dish. Cut the corn cobs into thick slices and add them to the dish. Mix all the ingredients for the spice mix together in a small bowl.

Brush the chicken and corn with the melted butter and sprinkle with the spice mix. Toss to coat well.

Cook the chicken over medium hot coals, turning occasionally, for 15 minutes, then add the corn slices and cook, turning occasionally, for a further 10–15 minutes, or until beginning to blacken slightly at the edges. Transfer to a large serving plate and serve immediately.

Rich, fruity sun-dried tomatoes perfectly complement the marinated turkey.

turkey with sun-dried tomato tapenade

4 turkey steaks

MARINADE
150 ml/5 fl oz white wine
1 tbsp white wine vinegar
1 tbsp olive oil
1 garlic clove, crushed
1 tbsp chopped fresh parsley
pepper

TAPENADE
225 g/8 oz sun-dried tomatoes
in oil, drained
4 canned anchovy fillets,
drained
1 garlic clove, crushed
1 tablespoon lemon juice
3 tablespoons chopped
fresh parsley

SERVES 4

Place the turkey steaks in a shallow, non-metallic dish. Mix all the marinade ingredients together in a jug, whisking well to mix. Pour the marinade over the turkey steaks, turning to coat. Cover with clingfilm and leave to marinate in the refrigerator for at least 1 hour.

Preheat the barbecue. To make the tapenade, put all the ingredients into a food processor and process to a smooth paste. Transfer to a bowl, cover with clingfilm and leave to chill in the refrigerator until required.

Drain the turkey steaks, reserving the marinade. Cook over medium hot coals for 10–15 minutes, turning and brushing frequently with the reserved marinade. Transfer to 4 large serving plates and top with the sun-dried tomato tapenade. Serve immediately.

The fine flavours of turkey and tarragon are complemented by the nutty-tasting bulgar.

turkey and tarragon burgers

55 g/2 oz bulgar wheat
salt and pepper
450 g/1 lb fresh turkey mince
1 tbsp finely grated orange rind
1 red onion, finely chopped
1 yellow pepper, deseeded,
peeled and finely chopped
25 g/1 oz toasted flaked
almonds
1 tbsp chopped fresh tarragon
1–2 tbsp sunflower oil

TO SERVE
lettuce leaves
2 large baked potatoes
tomato relish

SERVES 4

Cook the bulgar wheat in a saucepan of lightly salted boiling water for 10–15 minutes, or according to the packet instructions.

Drain the bulgar wheat and place in a bowl with the turkey mince, orange rind, onions, yellow pepper, almonds, tarragon and salt and pepper. Mix together, then shape into 4 equal-sized burgers. Cover and leave to chill for 1 hour.

Preheat the barbecue. Brush the burgers lightly with the oil and cook over hot coals for 5–6 minutes on each side or until cooked through.

Place a few lettuce leaves on 4 plates. Add the baked potato halves and top with the burgers. Spoon over a little tomato relish and serve.

The mustard coating on the poussins gives them a lovely orange-gold colour.

butterflied poussins

4 poussins,
about 450 g/1 lb each
1 tbsp paprika
1 tbsp mustard powder
1 tbsp ground cumin
pinch of cayenne pepper
1 tbsp tomato ketchup
1 tbsp lemon juice
salt
5 tbsp melted butter

TO GARNISH
fresh coriander sprigs

SERVES 4

To spatchcock the poussins, turn 1 bird breast-side down and, using strong kitchen scissors or poultry shears, cut through the skin and ribcage along both sides of the backbone, from tail to neck. Remove the backbone and turn the bird breast-side up. Press down firmly on the breastbone to flatten. Fold the wingtips underneath. Push a skewer through one wing, the top of the breast and out of the other wing. Push a second skewer through one thigh, the bottom of the breast and out through the other thigh. Repeat with the remaining poussins.

Mix the paprika, mustard powder, cumin, cayenne, tomato ketchup and lemon juice together in a small bowl and season to taste with salt. Gradually stir in the butter to make a smooth paste. Spread the paste evenly over the poussins, cover and leave to marinate in the refrigerator for up to 8 hours.

Preheat the barbecue. Cook the poussins over medium hot coals, turning frequently, for 25–30 minutes, brushing with a little oil if necessary. Transfer to a serving plate, garnish with fresh coriander sprigs and serve.

Apricots and onions counteract the richness of the duck.

fruity **duck**

4 duck breasts
115 g/4 oz ready-to-eat dried
apricots
2 shallots, thinly sliced
2 tbsp clear honey
1 tsp sesame oil
2 tsp Chinese five-spice powder

TO GARNISH
4 spring onions

SERVES 4

Preheat the barbecue. Using a sharp knife, cut a long slit in the fleshy side of each duck breast to make a pocket. Divide the apricots and shallots between the pockets and secure with skewers.

Mix the honey and sesame oil together in a small bowl and brush all over the duck. Sprinkle with the Chinese five-spice powder. To make the garnish, make a few cuts lengthways down the stem of each spring onion. Place in a bowl of ice-cold water and leave until the tassels open out. Drain well before using.

Cook the duck over medium hot coals for 6–8 minutes on each side. Remove the skewers, transfer to a large serving plate and garnish with the spring onion tassels. Serve immediately.

fabulous fish and seafood

Fresh fish and seafood are a delicious and healthy option. This chapter is packed with clever ideas for enhancing their flavour using appetising stuffings, mouthwatering marinades and aromatic herbs and spices. Recipes include inexpensive fish dishes for family lunches, simple grills for ease and speed and luxurious centrepieces for special occasions.

This spicy, Mexican-style tuna is sure to be a favourite with your adult guests.

mexican tuna

4 tuna steaks, about
175 g/6 oz each

SAUCE
2 tbsp corn oil
2 shallots, finely chopped
1 garlic clove, finely chopped
1 red pepper,
deseeded and chopped
2 beef tomatoes, chopped
3 tbsp tomato ketchup
2 tbsp mild mustard
2 tbsp muscovado sugar
1 tbsp clear Mexican honey
1 tbsp cayenne pepper
1 tbsp chilli powder
1 tbsp paprika
1 tbsp tequila

TO GARNISH
fresh coriander sprigs
lime wedges

SERVES 4

To make the sauce, heat the oil in a heavy-based saucepan. Add the shallots and garlic, and cook over a low heat, stirring occasionally, for 5 minutes, or until softened, but not coloured. Add the red pepper and cook for 1 minute, then add the tomatoes and simmer, stirring occasionally, for 20 minutes. Stir in the tomato ketchup, mustard, sugar, honey, cayenne, chilli powder, paprika and tequila and simmer for 20 minutes. Remove the saucepan from the heat and leave to cool.

Spoon the sauce into a food processor and process to a smooth purée. Rinse the fish under cold running water and pat dry with kitchen paper. Brush both sides of the tuna fillets with the sauce, place in a shallow dish, cover with clingfilm and leave to marinate in the refrigerator for 1 hour. Reserve the remaining sauce.

Preheat the barbecue. Brush the tuna steaks with the sauce and cook over medium hot coals, brushing frequently with the sauce, for 3 minutes on each side. Transfer to serving plates, garnish with fresh coriander sprigs and serve immediately with lime wedges.

Lightly spiced, these colourful kebabs look and taste delicious.

caribbean fish kebabs

1 kg/2 lb 4 oz swordfish steaks
3 tbsp olive oil
3 tbsp lime juice
1 garlic clove, finely chopped
1 tsp paprika
salt and pepper
3 onions, cut into wedges
6 tomatoes, cut into wedges

SERVES 6

Using a sharp knife, cut the fish into 2.5-cm/1-inch cubes and place in a shallow, non-metallic dish. Place the oil, lime juice, garlic and paprika in a jug and mix well. Season to taste with salt and pepper. Pour the marinade over the fish, turning to coat. Cover with clingfilm and leave to marinate in the refrigerator for 1 hour.

Preheat the barbecue. Thread the fish cubes, onion wedges and tomato wedges alternately on to 6 long, presoaked wooden skewers. Reserve the marinade.

Cook the kebabs over medium hot coals for 8–10 minutes, turning and brushing frequently with the reserved marinade. When they are cooked through, transfer the kebabs to a large serving plate and serve immediately.

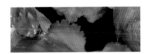

This classic Thai combination of flavours is perfect with all kinds of fish and seafood

coconut prawns

6 spring onions
400 ml/14 fl oz coconut milk
finely grated rind and juice
of 1 lime
4 tbsp chopped fresh coriander
2 tbsp corn or sunflower oil
pepper
650 g/1 lb 7 oz raw tiger prawns

TO GARNISH
lemon wedges
fresh coriander sprigs

SERVES 4

Finely chop the spring onions and place in a large, shallow, non-metallic dish with the coconut milk, lime rind and juice, coriander and oil. Mix well and season to taste with pepper. Add the prawns, turning to coat. Cover with clingfilm and leave to marinate in the refrigerator for 1 hour.

Preheat the barbecue. Drain the prawns, reserving the marinade. Thread the prawns on to 8 long metal skewers.

Cook the skewers over medium hot coals, brushing with the reserved marinade and turning frequently, for 8 minutes, or until they have changed colour. Cook the lemon wedges, skin-side down over medium hot coals, for the last 5 minutes. Serve the prawns immediately, garnished with the hot lemon wedges and coriander sprigs.

Meaty and succulent, monkfish is ideal for the barbecue.

orange and lemon peppered monkfish

2 oranges
2 lemons
2 monkfish tails, about
500 g/1 lb 2 oz each, skinned
and cut into 4 fillets
6 fresh lemon thyme sprigs
2 tbsp olive oil
salt
2 tbsp green peppercorns,
lightly crushed

TO GARNISH
orange wedges
lemon wedges

SERVES 6

Cut 8 orange slices and 8 lemon slices, reserving the remaining fruit. Rinse the monkfish fillets under cold running water and pat dry with kitchen paper. Place 1 fillet from each monkfish tail, cut-side up, on a work surface and divide the citrus slices between them. Top with the lemon thyme. Reassemble the tails and tie them securely together at intervals with kitchen string or trussing thread. Place the tails in a large, shallow, non-metallic dish.

Squeeze the juice from the remaining fruit and mix with the olive oil in a jug. Season to taste with salt, then spoon the mixture over the fish. Cover with clingfilm and leave to marinate in the refrigerator for up to 1 hour, spooning the marinade over the fish tails once or twice.

Preheat the barbecue. Drain the monkfish tails, reserving the marinade. Sprinkle the crushed green peppercorns over the fish, pressing them in with your fingers. Cook the monkfish over medium hot coals, turning and brushing frequently with the reserved marinade, for 20–25 minutes. Transfer to a chopping board, remove and discard the string and cut the monkfish tails into slices. Serve immediately, garnished with orange and lemon wedges.

Delicate flavours make these prawns a real barbecue treat.

oriental prawn skewers

MARINADE
100 ml/3¹/₂ fl oz vegetable oil
2 tbsp chilli oil
50 ml/2 fl oz lemon juice
1 tbsp rice wine or sherry
2 spring onions, trimmed and
finely chopped
2 garlic cloves, finely chopped
1 tbsp grated fresh root ginger
1 tbsp chopped
fresh lemon grass
2 tbsp chopped fresh coriander
salt and pepper

SKEWERS
1 kg/2 lb 4 oz large prawns,
peeled and deveined, but with
tails left on

TO GARNISH
wedges of lemon
chopped fresh chives

TO SERVE
freshly cooked jasmine rice

SERVES 4

Put the oils, lemon juice, rice wine or sherry, spring onions, garlic, ginger, lemon grass and coriander into a food processor and season well with salt and pepper. Process until smooth, then transfer to a non-metallic (glass or ceramic) bowl, which will not react with acid.

Add the prawns to the bowl and turn them in the mixture until they are well coated. Cover with clingfilm and place in the refrigerator to marinate for at least 2 hours.

When the prawns are thoroughly marinated, lift them out and thread them onto skewers, leaving a small space at either end. Barbecue them with the lemon wedges over hot coals for 4–5 minutes, or until cooked right through (but do not overcook), turning them frequently and basting with the remaining marinade. Arrange the skewers on a bed of freshly cooked jasmine rice. Garnish with the lemon wedges and chopped fresh chives.

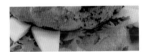

Tuna is an excellent choice for barbecues, as it doesn't break up during cooking.

fresh tuna burgers with mango salsa

225 g/8 oz sweet potatoes, chopped
salt
450 g/1 lb fresh tuna steaks
6 spring onions, finely chopped
175 g/6 oz courgette, grated
1 fresh red jalapeño chilli, deseeded and finely chopped
2 tbsp prepared mango chutney
1 tbsp sunflower oil

MANGO SALSA
1 large ripe mango, peeled and stoned
2 ripe tomatoes, finely chopped
4-cm/1^{1}/2-inch piece cucumber, finely diced
1 fresh red jalapeño chilli, deseeded and finely chopped
1 tbsp chopped fresh coriander
1–2 tsp clear honey

TO SERVE
salad leaves
4–6 slices of corn bread, halved

SERVES 4–6

Cook the sweet potatoes in a saucepan of lightly salted boiling water for 15–20 minutes, or until tender. Drain well, then mash and place in a food processor. Cut the tuna into chunks and add to the potatoes.

Add the spring onions, courgette, chilli and mango chutney to the food processor and, using the pulse button, blend together. Shape into 4–6 equal-sized burgers, then cover and leave to chill for 1 hour.

Meanwhile make the salsa. Slice the mango flesh, reserving 8 good slices for serving. Finely chop the remainder, then mix with the tomatoes, cucumber, chilli, coriander and honey. Mix well, then spoon into a small bowl. Cover and leave for 30 minutes to allow the flavours to develop.

When the barbecue is hot, add the burgers and cook over medium hot coals for 4–6 minutes on each side or until piping hot.

Place some salad leaves on one half of each piece of corn bread, top with the slices of reserved mango, then the burger. Spoon over a little salsa and serve with the other half of the bread.

An unusual but delicious treat, with a spicy Oriental flavour.

thai crab burgers with beansprouts

1¹/₂ tbsp sunflower oil
1 fresh red chilli, deseeded and
finely chopped
2.5-cm/1-inch piece fresh root
ginger, grated
2 lemon grass stalks, outer
leaves removed and finely
chopped
350 g/12 oz canned white
crabmeat, drained and flaked
225 g/8 oz cooked peeled
prawns, thawed if frozen and
squeezed dry
175 g/6 oz cooked Thai rice
1 tbsp chopped fresh coriander
115 g/4 oz beansprouts
6 spring onions, finely chopped
1 tbsp soy sauce
1–2 tbsp wholemeal flour

TO SERVE
shredded Chinese leaves
fresh beansprouts
4 hamburger buns
sweet chilli sauce

SERVES 4

Heat a wok or frying pan and when hot add 2 teaspoons of the oil, the chilli, ginger and lemon grass and stir-fry over a medium-high heat for 1 minute. Remove the wok from the heat and leave to cool.

Place the chilli mixture, crabmeat, prawns, rice, chopped coriander, beansprouts, spring onions and soy sauce in a food processor and, using the pulse button, blend together. Shape into 4 equal-sized burgers, then coat in the flour. Cover and leave to chill for 1 hour.

Preheat barbecue. Brush the burgers lightly with the remaining oil and cook over hot coals for 3–4 minutes on each side or until piping hot.

Place some shredded Chinese leaves and beansprouts on top of the bases of the hamburger buns, top with the burgers and drizzle over a little sweet chilli sauce. Place the lid in position and serve.

The sweet but piquant sauce complements the richness of the salmon superbly.

salmon teriyaki

4 salmon fillets,
about 175 g/6 oz each

SAUCE
1 tbsp cornflour
125 ml/4 fl oz dark soy sauce
4 tbsp mirin
or medium-dry sherry
2 tbsp rice or cider vinegar
2 tbsp clear honey

TO SERVE
1/2 cucumber
mixed salad leaves,
torn into pieces
4 spring onions, thinly sliced
diagonally

SERVES 4

Rinse the salmon fillets under cold running water, pat dry with kitchen paper and place in a large, shallow, non-metallic dish. To make the sauce, mix the cornflour and soy sauce together in a jug until a smooth paste forms, then stir in the remaining ingredients. Pour three-quarters of the sauce over the salmon, turning to coat. Cover with clingfilm and leave to marinate in the refrigerator for 2 hours.

Preheat the barbecue. Cut the cucumber into batons, then arrange the salad leaves, cucumber and spring onions on 4 serving plates. Pour the remaining sauce into a saucepan and set over the barbecue to warm through.

Remove the salmon fillets from the dish and reserve the marinade. Cook the salmon over medium hot coals, brushing frequently with the reserved marinade, for 3–4 minutes on each side. Transfer the salmon fillets to the prepared serving plates and pour the warmed sauce over them. Serve immediately.

This magnificent dish will form the centrepiece of a special occasion barbecue.

caribbean sea bass

1.5 kg/3 lb 5 oz sea bass,
cleaned and scaled
1–2 tsp olive oil
1 tsp saffron powder
salt and pepper
$^{1}/_{2}$ lemon, sliced,
plus extra to garnish
1 lime, sliced,
plus extra to garnish
1 bunch of fresh thyme

SERVES 6

Preheat the barbecue. Rinse the sea bass inside and out under cold running water, then pat dry with kitchen paper. Using a sharp knife, make a series of shallow diagonal slashes along each side of the fish. Brush each slash with a little olive oil, then sprinkle over the saffron powder.

Brush a large fish basket with olive oil and place the fish in the basket, but do not close it. Season the cavity with salt and pepper. Place the lemon and lime slices and the thyme in the cavity without overfilling it.

Close the basket and cook the fish over medium hot coals for 10 minutes on each side. Carefully transfer to a large serving plate, garnish with lemon and lime slices and serve immediately.

Delicious tuna steaks are served with a colourful and spicy chilli salsa.

chargrilled tuna with chilli salsa

4 tuna steaks,
about 175 g/6 oz each
grated rind and juice of 1 lime
2 tbsp olive oil
salt and pepper

CHILLI SALSA
2 orange peppers
1 tbsp olive oil
juice of 1 lime
juice of 1 orange
2–3 fresh red chillies, deseeded
and chopped
pinch of cayenne pepper

TO GARNISH
fresh coriander sprigs

SERVES 4

Rinse the tuna thoroughly under cold running water and pat dry with kitchen paper, then place in a large, shallow, non-metallic dish. Sprinkle the lime rind and juice and the olive oil over the fish. Season to taste with salt and pepper, cover with clingfilm and leave to marinate in the refrigerator for up to 1 hour.

Preheat the barbecue. To make the salsa, brush the peppers with the olive oil and cook over hot coals, turning frequently, for 10 minutes, or until the skin is blackened and charred. Remove from the barbecue and leave to cool slightly, then peel off the skins and discard the seeds. Put the peppers into a food processor with the remaining salsa ingredients and process to a purée. Transfer to a bowl and season to taste with salt and pepper.

Cook the tuna over hot coals for 4–5 minutes on each side, until golden. Transfer to serving plates, garnish with coriander sprigs and serve with the salsa.

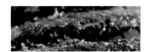

Fabulously fresh sardines are stuffed with herbs and coated in a mild spice mixture.

stuffed sardines

15 g/¹/₂ oz fresh parsley,
finely chopped
4 garlic cloves, finely chopped
12 fresh sardines,
cleaned and scaled
3 tbsp lemon juice
85 g/3 oz plain flour
1 tsp ground cumin
salt and pepper
olive oil, for brushing

SERVES 6

Place the parsley and garlic in a bowl and mix together. Rinse the fish inside and out under cold running water and pat dry with kitchen paper. Spoon the herb mixture into the fish cavities and pat the remainder all over the outside of the fish. Sprinkle the sardines with lemon juice and transfer to a large, shallow, non-metallic dish. Cover with clingfilm and leave to marinate in the refrigerator for 1 hour.

Preheat the barbecue. Mix the flour and ground cumin together in a bowl, then season to taste with salt and pepper. Spread out the seasoned flour on a large plate and gently roll the sardines in the flour to coat.

Brush the sardines with olive oil and cook over medium hot coals for 3–4 minutes on each side. Serve immediately.

 Fresh fish is made extra special with the addition of Indonesian-style spices.

baked red mullet

4 banana leaves
2 limes
3 garlic cloves
4 red mullet,
about 350 g/12 oz each
2 spring onions, thinly sliced
2.5-cm/1-inch piece
fresh root ginger
1 onion, finely chopped
4 1/2 tsp groundnut or corn oil
3 tbsp kecap manis
or light soy sauce
1 tsp ground coriander
1 tsp ground cumin
1/4 tsp ground cloves
1/4 tsp ground turmeric

SERVES 4

Preheat the barbecue. If necessary, cut the banana leaves into 4 x 40-cm/ 16-inch squares, using a sharp knife or scissors. Thinly slice 1/2 a lime and 1 garlic clove. Clean and scale the fish, then rinse it inside and out under cold running water. Pat dry with kitchen paper. Using a sharp knife, make a series of deep diagonal slashes on the side of each fish, then insert the lime and garlic slices into the slashes. Place the fish on the banana leaf squares and sprinkle with the spring onions. Alternatively, wrap the fish in foil.

Finely chop the remaining garlic and squeeze the juice from the remaining limes. Finely chop the ginger, then place the garlic in a bowl with the onion, ginger, oil, kecap manis, spices and lime juice and mix to a paste.

Spoon the paste into the fish cavities and spread it over the outside. Roll up the parcels and tie securely with string. Cook over medium hot coals, turning occasionally, for 15–20 minutes. Serve.

Seafood brochettes always look attractive and are perennially popular.

mixed seafood brochettes

2 tbsp sesame seeds
500 g/1 lb 2 oz swordfish steaks
or monkfish fillet
350 ml/12 fl oz dry white wine
2 tbsp corn or sunflower oil
grated rind and juice of 2 limes
2 garlic cloves, finely chopped
salt and pepper
1¹/₂ tsp cornflour
2 tbsp water
2 tbsp chopped fresh coriander
12 prepared scallops
12 raw tiger prawns

SERVES 6

Dry-fry the sesame seeds in a covered heavy-based frying pan until they begin to pop and give off their aroma. Remove from the heat and reserve. Cut the fish into 2.5-cm/1-inch cubes, then place in a shallow, non-metallic dish. Mix 200 ml/7 fl oz of the wine, the oil, lime rind and juice and garlic together in a jug and season to taste with salt and pepper. Pour half of this over the fish, turning to coat, and pour the remainder into a small saucepan. Cover the fish with clingfilm and leave to marinate in a cool place or the refrigerator for up to 1 hour.

Preheat the barbecue. Set the saucepan over a low heat and add the remaining wine. Mix the cornflour and water into a smooth paste and stir it into the saucepan, then bring to the boil, stirring constantly, and simmer until thickened. Remove the saucepan from the heat and stir in the coriander and roasted sesame seeds. Cover with a lid and place by the side of the barbecue to keep warm.

Remove the fish from the marinade and thread on to 6 metal skewers, alternating with the scallops and prawns. Cook the brochettes over medium hot coals, turning occasionally, for 5–8 minutes, or until the fish is cooked and the prawns have changed colour. Transfer to a large serving plate and serve immediately with the sauce.

This classic combination is delicious cooked on the barbecue.

bacon-wrapped trout

4 trout, cleaned
4 smoked streaky bacon
rashers, rinded
4 tbsp plain flour
salt and pepper
2 tbsp olive oil
2 tbsp lemon juice

TO GARNISH
fresh parsley sprigs
lemon wedges

TO SERVE
lamb's lettuce

SERVES 4

Preheat the barbecue. Rinse the trout inside and out under cold running water and pat dry with kitchen paper. Stretch the bacon using the back of a heavy, flat-bladed knife.

Season the flour with salt and pepper and spread it out on a large, flat plate. Gently roll each trout in the seasoned flour until thoroughly coated. Beginning just below the head, wrap a rasher of bacon in a spiral along the length of each fish.

Brush the trout with olive oil and cook over medium hot coals for 5–8 minutes on each side. Transfer to 4 large serving plates and drizzle with the lemon juice. Garnish with parsley and lemon wedges and serve with lamb's lettuce.

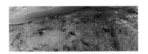

These spicy burgers combine fragrant Thai flavours with delicate white fish.

thai fish burgers

350 g/12 oz haddock fillets, skinned and cut into small pieces
25 g/1 oz almonds, chopped
25 g/1 oz fresh breadcrumbs
1/2 onion, finely chopped
1 red chilli, deseeded and finely chopped
1 egg white
1 tbsp soy sauce
1 tbsp finely chopped lemon grass
2 tbsp chopped fresh coriander
1 tbsp groundnut oil

TO SERVE
4 hamburger buns
slices of tomato
green salad leaves

SERVES 4

Put the haddock, almonds, breadcrumbs, onion, chilli, egg white, soy sauce, lemon grass and coriander into a large bowl and stir together. Put the mixture into a food processor and process until thoroughly blended. Transfer to a clean work surface and, using your hands, shape the mixture into flat, round burger shapes.

Preheat barbecue. Brush the burgers lightly with the oil and cook over hot coals for 2–3 minutes on each side or until cooked through.

Remove from the heat. Serve with hamburger buns stuffed with tomato slices and crisp lettuce, and a green side salad.

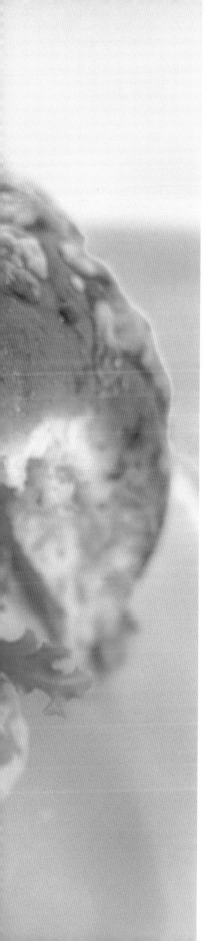

veggie heaven

Although a barbecue tends to be a meat-orientated feast, this chapter proves that vegetarians need not feel left out. Vegetarian food is diverse and versatile, and works extremely well when cooked on the barbecue. This section provides some delicious vegetarian dishes that will tempt even the most hardened of carnivores.

These tasty sandwiches make a delicious meal when served with bread and salad.

aubergine and mozzarella sandwiches

1 large aubergine
1 tbsp lemon juice
3 tbsp olive oil
salt and pepper
125 g/4$\frac{1}{2}$ oz grated
mozzarella cheese
2 sun-dried tomatoes, chopped

TO SERVE
Italian bread
mixed salad leaves
tomato slices

SERVES 2

Preheat the barbecue. Using a sharp knife, slice the aubergine into thin rounds.

Mix the lemon juice and olive oil together in a small bowl and season the mixture with salt and pepper to taste. Brush the aubergine slices with the olive oil and lemon juice mixture and cook over medium hot coals for 2–3 minutes, without turning, until golden on the underside.

Turn half of the aubergine slices over and sprinkle with cheese and chopped sun-dried tomatoes.

Place the remaining aubergine slices on top of the cheese and tomatoes, turning them so that the pale side is uppermost. Barbecue for 1–2 minutes, then carefully turn the whole sandwich over and barbecue for a further 1–2 minutes. Baste with the olive oil mixture.

Serve with Italian bread, mixed salad leaves and a few slices of tomato.

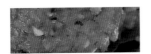

You can, if you like, substitute the flageolet beans for black-eyed or red kidney beans.

the ultimate vegetarian burger

85 g/3 oz brown rice
salt and pepper
400 g/14 oz canned flageolet beans, drained
115 g/4 oz unsalted cashew nuts
3 garlic cloves
1 red onion, cut into wedges
115 g/4 oz sweetcorn kernels
2 tbsp tomato purée
1 tbsp chopped fresh oregano
2 tbsp wholemeal flour
2 tbsp sunflower oil

TO SERVE
shredded lettuce
4–6 wholemeal burger buns
slices of tomato
4–6 slices halloumi cheese

SERVES 4–6

Preheat the barbecue. Cook the rice in a saucepan of lightly salted boiling water for 20 minutes, or until tender. Drain and place in a food processor.

Add the beans, cashew nuts, garlic, onion, sweetcorn, tomato purée, oregano and salt and pepper to the rice in the food processor and, using the pulse button, blend together. Shape into 4–6 equal-sized burgers, then coat in the flour. Cover and leave to chill for 1 hour.

Lightly brush the burgers with oil. When the barbecue is hot cook the burgers over medium hot coals for 5–6 minutes on each side or until cooked and piping hot.

Place some shredded lettuce on top of the bases of the hamburger buns and top with the burgers. Add the tomato and cheese slices, and place under a grill for 1–2 minutes to melt the cheese if desired. Serve.

Vegetarian sausages are no longer the poor relation with a recipe full of flavour and inspiration.

spicy vegetarian sausages

1 garlic clove, finely chopped
1 onion, finely chopped
1 red chilli, deseeded and finely chopped
400 g/14 oz canned red kidney beans, rinsed, drained and mashed
100 g/3¹/₂ oz fresh breadcrumbs
50 g/1³/₄ oz almonds, toasted and ground
50 g/1³/₄ oz cooked rice
50 g/1³/₄ oz Cheddar cheese, grated
1 egg yolk
1 tbsp chopped fresh oregano
salt and pepper
flour, for dusting
vegetable oil, for brushing

TO SERVE
fresh finger rolls
sliced onion, lightly cooked
sliced tomato, lightly cooked
tomato ketchup and/or mustard

SERVES 4

Put the garlic, onion, chilli, mashed kidney beans, breadcrumbs, almonds, rice and cheese into a large bowl. Stir in the egg yolk and oregano, then season with salt and plenty of pepper.

Using your hands, form the mixture into sausage shapes. Roll each sausage in a little flour, then transfer to a bowl, cover with clingfilm and refrigerate for 45 minutes.

Brush a piece of aluminium foil with oil, then put the sausages on the foil and brush them with a little more vegetable oil. Transfer the sausages and foil to the barbecue. Barbecue over hot coals, turning the sausages frequently, for about 15 minutes or until cooked right through. Serve with finger rolls, cooked sliced onion and tomato, and tomato ketchup and or mustard.

Halloumi is just perfect for the barbecue and these kebabs are bursting with colour and taste.

halloumi cheese and vegetable kebabs

MARINADE
4 tbsp extra-virgin olive oil
2 tbsp balsamic vinegar
2 garlic cloves, finely chopped
1 tbsp chopped fresh coriander
salt and pepper

KEBABS
225 g/8 oz halloumi cheese
12 button mushrooms
8 baby onions
12 cherry tomatoes
2 courgettes,
cut into small chunks
1 red pepper, deseeded and cut
into small chunks

TO GARNISH
chopped fresh coriander

TO SERVE
freshly cooked rice
or salad leaves
fresh crusty bread

SERVES 4

Put the oil, vinegar, garlic and coriander into a large bowl. Season with salt and pepper and mix until well combined.

Cut the halloumi cheese into bite-sized cubes. Thread the cubes onto skewers, alternating them with whole button mushrooms, baby onions, cherry tomatoes, and courgette and red pepper chunks. When the skewers are full (leave a small space at either end), transfer them to the bowl and turn them in the mixture until they are well coated. Cover with clingfilm and place in the refrigerator to marinate for at least 2 hours.

When the skewers are thoroughly marinated, barbecue them over hot coals for 5–10 minutes or until they are cooked to your taste, turning them frequently and basting with the remaining marinade. Arrange the skewers on a bed of freshly cooked rice or fresh mixed salad leaves, garnish with coriander leaves and serve with fresh crusty bread.

Blue cheese, apples and nuts are a winning combination in this fabulous burger.

blue cheese and apple burgers

175 g/6 oz new potatoes
225 g/8 oz mixed nuts, such as pecans, almonds and hazelnuts
1 onion, roughly chopped
225 g/8 oz Granny Smith or other eating apples, peeled, cored and grated
175 g/6 oz blue cheese, such as Stilton, crumbled
55 g/2 oz fresh wholemeal breadcrumbs
salt and pepper
2 tbsp wholemeal flour
1–2 tbsp sunflower oil

TO SERVE
salad leaves
4–6 hamburger buns
slices of red onion

SERVES 4–6

Cook the potatoes in a saucepan of boiling water for 15–20 minutes, or until tender when pierced with a fork. Drain and, using a potato masher, crush into small pieces. Place in a large bowl.

Place the nuts and onion in a food processor and, using the pulse button, chop finely. Add the nuts, onion, apple, cheese and breadcrumbs to the potatoes in the bowl. Season with salt and pepper to taste. Mix well, then shape into 4–6 equal-sized burgers. Coat in the flour, then cover and leave to chill for 1 hour.

Preheat barbecue. Brush the burgers lightly with the oil and cook over hot coals for 5–6 minutes on each side or until piping hot.

Place the salad leaves on top of the bases of the hamburger buns and top with the burgers. Add the slices of red onion and serve.

Mushrooms and pears make a unique combination for these tasty skewers.

vegetarian mushroom and pear skewers

MARINADE
2 tbsp extra-virgin olive oil
1 tbsp balsamic vinegar
1 garlic clove, finely chopped
salt and pepper

SKEWERS
750 g/1 lb 10 oz mycroprotein
(Quorn) pieces or fillets
(cut into small chunks)
450 g/1 lb button mushrooms
1 large pear, cored and cut into
small chunks

TO SERVE
fresh green and red
lettuce leaves
fresh crusty bread

TO GARNISH
wedges of pear

SERVES 4

Put the oil, vinegar and garlic into a large bowl. Season with salt and pepper and mix until well combined.

Thread the mycroprotein (Quorn) pieces onto skewers, alternating them with the mushrooms and pear chunks. When the skewers are full (leave a small space at either end), transfer them to the bowl and turn them in the mixture until they are well coated. Cover with clingfilm and place in the refrigerator to marinate for at least 1 hour.

Barbecue the skewers over hot coals for about 5 minutes, or until the mycroprotein is cooked right through, turning them frequently and basting with the remaining marinade. Arrange the skewers on a bed of fresh green and red lettuce leaves, garnish with wedges of pear and serve with fresh crusty bread.

Tofu is made from soya beans and will easily absorb any flavour it is combined with.

vegetable and tofu burger

115 g/4 oz Thai rice
115 g/4 oz carrot, grated
6 spring onions,
roughly chopped
55 g/2 oz unsalted peanuts
85 g/3 oz fresh beansprouts
225 g/8 oz firm tofu (drained
weight), finely chopped
1 tsp prepared ginger pulp
$^1/_2$–1 tsp crushed chillies
1–2 tbsp sunflower oil

TO SERVE
shredded pak choi
fresh beansprouts
4–6 hamburger buns
oyster and shiitake mushrooms,
lightly sautéed
satay sauce

SERVES 4–6

Cook the rice in a saucepan of lightly boiling water for 12–15 minutes, or until soft. Drain and place in a large bowl.

Place the carrot, spring onions and peanuts in a food processor and, using the pulse button, chop finely. Add the rice, beansprouts, tofu, ginger and chillies and blend together. Shape into 4–6 equal-sized burgers, firmly pressing them together. Cover and leave to chill for 1 hour.

Preheat the barbecue. Brush the burgers lightly with the oil and cook over hot coals for 5–6 minutes on each side or until piping hot.

Place some shredded pak choi and beansprouts on top of the bases of the hamburger buns and top with the burgers. Add the sautéed mushrooms and drizzle over a little satay sauce. Place the lid in position and serve.

Bring a taste of the tropics to your barbecue with these sizzling kebabs.

spicy caribbean kebabs

KEBABS
1 corn cob
1 christophene, peeled and cut into chunks
1 ripe plantain, peeled and cut into thick slices
1 aubergine, cut into chunks
1 red pepper, deseeded and cut into chunks
1 green pepper, deseeded and cut into chunks
1 onion, cut into wedges
8 button mushrooms
4 cherry tomatoes

MARINADE
150 ml/5 fl oz tomato juice
4 tbsp sunflower oil
4 tbsp lime juice
3 tbsp dark soy sauce
1 shallot, finely chopped
2 garlic cloves, finely chopped
1 fresh green chilli, deseeded and finely chopped
$1/2$ tsp ground cinnamon
pepper

SERVES 4

Using a sharp knife, remove the husks and silks from the corn cob and cut into 2.5-cm/1-inch thick slices. Blanch the christophene chunks in boiling water for 2 minutes. Drain, refresh under cold running water and drain again. Place the christophene chunks in a large bowl with the corn cob slices and the remaining kebab ingredients.

Mix all the marinade ingredients together in a jug, seasoning to taste with pepper. Pour the marinade over the vegetables, tossing to coat. Cover with clingfilm and leave to marinate in the refrigerator for 3 hours.

Preheat the barbecue. Drain the vegetables, reserving the marinade. Thread the vegetables on to several metal skewers. Cook over hot coals, turning and brushing frequently with the reserved marinade, for 10–15 minutes. Transfer to a large serving plate and serve immediately.

Mild, sweet onions and salty cheese create an inspiring combination of flavour and texture.

cheese and red onion kebabs

3 red onions
450 g/1 lb halloumi cheese, cut into 2.5-cm/1-inch cubes
2 tart eating apples, cored and cut into wedges

MARINADE
4 tbsp olive oil
1 tbsp cider vinegar
1 tbsp Dijon mustard
1 garlic clove, finely chopped
1 tsp finely chopped sage
salt and pepper

SERVES 4

Cut the onions into wedges, then place in a large, shallow, non-metallic dish with the cheese and apples. Mix the oil, vinegar, mustard, garlic and sage together in a jug and season to taste with salt and pepper.

Pour the marinade over the onions, cheese and apples, tossing to coat. Cover with clingfilm and leave to marinate in the refrigerator for 2 hours.

Preheat the barbecue. Drain the onions, cheese and apples, reserving the marinade. Thread the onions, cheese and apples alternately on to several metal skewers. Cook over hot coals, turning and brushing frequently with the reserved marinade, for 10–15 minutes. Transfer to a large serving plate and serve immediately.

This classic dish will be popular with vegetarians and non-vegetarians alike.

stuffed mushrooms

12 open-cap mushrooms
4 tsp olive oil
4 spring onions, chopped
100 g/3^1/$_2$ oz fresh brown breadcrumbs
1 tsp chopped fresh oregano
100 g/3^1/$_2$ oz feta cheese, crumbled

MAKES 12

Preheat the barbecue. Remove the stalks from the mushrooms and chop the stalks finely. Heat half of the olive oil in a large frying pan. Add the mushroom stalks and spring onions and sauté briefly.

Place the sautéed mushroom stalks and spring onions in a large bowl. Add the breadcrumbs and oregano, mix well, then incorporate the crumbled feta. Spoon the stuffing mixture into the mushroom caps.

Drizzle the olive oil over the stuffed mushrooms, then cook on an oiled rack over medium hot coals for 8–10 minutes. Transfer the mushrooms to individual serving plates and serve while still hot.

These filled baps make great food for an informal party outdoors.

cheese and vegetable baps

2 red peppers, deseeded and cut into quarters
2 courgettes, trimmed and sliced
1 large onion, cut into rings
150 g/5¹/₂ oz baby corn
3 tbsp olive oil
4 large white or wholemeal baps, halved horizontally to make 8 thinner rounds
115 g/4 oz smoked firm cheese, such as Applewood, grated

TO SERVE
soured cream

SERVES 4

Cook the peppers on the barbecue, skin–side down, for 5 minutes or until the skins are charred. Transfer them to a polythene bag, seal the bag and set to one side. Brush the courgettes, onion rings and corn with oil and barbecue over hot coals for 5 minutes, turning them frequently and basting with more oil if necessary.

While the vegetables are on the barbecue, take the bottom halves of the baps, brush the cut sides with oil and sprinkle over some cheese. Cover with the top halves, then wrap each bap in foil and transfer them to the barbecue. Warm for 2–4 minutes, just until the cheese starts to melt (do not overcook).

While the baps are warming, take the pepper quarters from the bag and remove the skins. Chop the flesh into small pieces and transfer it to a plate with the other vegetables.

Transfer the baps to serving plates and remove the foil. Fill them with the cooked vegetables and soured cream and serve at once.

If you prefer a chunkier texture, blend the mixture only briefly and do not peel the peppers.

yam and red pepper burgers

225 g/8 oz yam, peeled and cut into chunks
salt and pepper
400 g/14 oz canned chickpeas, drained
2 red peppers, deseeded and peeled
2–3 garlic cloves, crushed
85 g/3 oz stoned black olives
2 tbsp sesame seeds
1 tbsp chopped fresh coriander
2 tbsp wholemeal flour
2 tbsp sunflower oil

TO SERVE
salad leaves
4–6 hamburger buns
hummus
tomato salsa

SERVES 4–6

Cook the yam in a saucepan of lightly salted boiling water for 15–20 minutes, or until tender. Drain well and place in a food processor.

Add the chickpeas, red peppers, garlic, olives, sesame seeds, coriander, and salt and pepper to the yam in the food processor and, using the pulse button, blend together. Shape into 4–6 equal-sized burgers, then coat in the flour. Cover and leave to chill for 1 hour. Preheat the barbecue.

Lightly brush the burgers with oil. When the barbecue is heated, add the burgers and cook over medium hot coals for 5–6 minutes on each side or until cooked and piping hot.

Place the salad leaves on top of the bases of the hamburger buns and top with the burgers. Spoon over a little hummus and tomato salsa. Place the lid in position and serve.

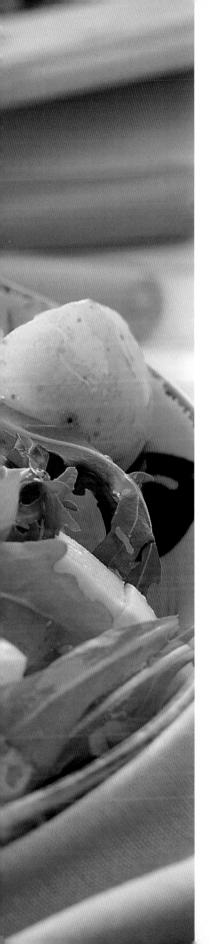

on the side

No barbecue would be complete without a
selection of delicious accompaniments to
complement the main meat, fish and vegetable
dishes. This chapter contains a range of fabulous
side dishes – from tasty potatoes to vibrant salads,
appetising dips and other barbecue classics – all of
which are sure to go down well with your guests.

This juicy corn on the cob is served with a fresh herb butter for extra flavour.

corn on the cob

4 corn cobs, with husks

HERB BUTTER
100 g/3¹/₂ oz butter
1 tbsp chopped fresh parsley
1 tsp chopped fresh chives
1 tsp chopped fresh thyme
grated rind of 1 lemon
salt and pepper

SERVES 4

Preheat the barbecue. To prepare the corn cobs, peel back the husks and remove the silken hairs. Fold back the husks and secure them in place with string if necessary.

Blanch the corn cobs in a large saucepan of boiling water for 5 minutes. Remove the corn cobs with a slotted spoon and drain thoroughly. Cook the corn cobs over medium hot coals for 20–30 minutes, turning frequently.

Meanwhile, soften the butter and beat in the parsley, chives, thyme, lemon rind and salt and pepper to taste. Transfer the corn cobs to serving plates, remove the string and pull back the husks. Serve each with a generous portion of herb butter.

 These mouthwatering potato slices are an excellent accompaniment to barbecued foods.

spicy sweet potato slices

450 g/1 lb sweet potatoes
2 tbsp sunflower oil
1 tsp chilli sauce
salt and pepper

SERVES 4

Preheat the barbecue. Bring a large saucepan of water to the boil. Add the sweet potatoes and parboil them for 10 minutes. Drain thoroughly and transfer to a chopping board. Allow to cool. Peel the potatoes and cut them into thick slices.

Mix the sunflower oil, chilli sauce and salt and pepper to taste together in a small bowl. Brush the spicy mixture liberally over one side of the potatoes. Place the potatoes, oil-side down, over medium hot coals and cook for 5–6 minutes.

Lightly brush the tops of the potatoes with the oil, turn them over and barbecue for a further 5 minutes, or until crisp and golden. Transfer the potatoes to a warmed serving dish and serve immediately.

Crispy potato skins make a delicious and moreish side dish.

crispy potato skins

8 small baking potatoes, scrubbed
50 g/1³/₄ oz butter, melted
salt and pepper

OPTIONAL TOPPING
6 spring onions, sliced
50 g/1³/₄ oz grated Gruyère cheese
50 g/1³/₄ oz salami, cut into thin strips

SERVES 4–6

Preheat the oven to 200°C/400°F/Gas Mark 6. Prick the potatoes with a fork and bake for 1 hour, or until tender. Alternatively, cook in a microwave on High for 12–15 minutes. Cut the potatoes in half and scoop out the flesh, leaving about 5 mm/¼ inch potato flesh lining the skin.

Preheat the barbecue. Brush the insides of the potato with melted butter.

Place the skins, cut-side down, over medium hot coals and cook for 10–15 minutes. Turn the potato skins over and barbecue for a further 5 minutes, or until they are crispy. Take care that they do not burn. Season the potato skins with salt and pepper to taste and serve while they are still warm.

If wished, the skins can be filled with a variety of toppings. Barbecue the potato skins as above for 10 minutes, then turn cut-side up and sprinkle with slices of spring onion, grated cheese and chopped salami. Barbecue for a further 5 minutes, or until the cheese begins to melt. Serve hot.

A popular accompaniment to barbecued meat, vegetable and fish dishes.

warm potatoes with pesto

450 g/1 lb small new potatoes
3 tsp pesto sauce
salt and pepper
25 g/1 oz fresh grated
Parmesan cheese

SERVES 4

Cook the potatoes in salted boiling water for about 15 minutes, or until tender. Drain, put in a salad bowl and allow to cool slightly.

Add the pesto, salt and pepper to the potatoes and toss together. Sprinkle with the Parmesan cheese and serve warm.

This classic salad is a perfect addition to any barbecue menu.

chef's salad

1 iceberg lettuce, shredded
175 g/6 oz cooked ham,
cut into thin strips
175 g/6 oz cooked tongue,
cut into thin strips
350 g/12 oz cooked chicken,
cut into thin strips
175 g/6 oz Gruyère cheese
4 tomatoes
3 hard-boiled eggs
400 ml/14 fl oz
Thousand Island Dressing

SERVES 6

Arrange the lettuce on a large serving platter. Arrange the cold meat decoratively on top.

Cut the Gruyère cheese into batons, quarter the tomatoes, and shell and quarter the hard-boiled eggs.

Arrange the cheese batons over the salad, and the tomato and egg quarters around the edge of the platter. Serve the salad immediately, and serve the dressing separately.

A delicious combination of ingredients makes this a fresh and appealing salad.

potato, rocket and mozzarella salad

650 g/1 lb 7 oz
small new potatoes
125 g/4¹/2 oz rocket leaves
150 g/5¹/2 oz firm mozzarella
1 large pear
1 tbsp lemon juice
salt and pepper

DRESSING
3 tbsp extra-virgin olive oil
1¹/2 tbsp white wine vinegar
1 tsp sugar
pinch of mustard powder

SERVES 4

Bring a saucepan of salted water to the boil. Add the potatoes, reduce the heat and cook for about 15 minutes, or until tender. Remove from the heat, drain and set aside to cool.

When the potatoes are cool, halve them and place them in a large salad bowl. Wash and drain the rocket leaves, cut the mozzarella into cubes, and wash, trim and slice the pear. Add them to the bowl along with the lemon juice. Season with salt and pepper.

To make the dressing, mix together the oil, vinegar, sugar and mustard powder. Pour the dressing over the salad and toss all the ingredients together until they are well coated. Serve at once.

The tantalising mix of flavours, textures and colours makes this salad a popular choice.

tomato, mozzarella and avocado salad

2 ripe beef tomatoes
150 g/5^1/$_2$ oz fresh
mozzarella cheese
2 avocados
4 tbsp olive oil
1^1/$_2$ tbsp white wine vinegar
1 tsp coarse grain mustard
salt and pepper
few fresh basil leaves,
torn into pieces
20 black olives

TO SERVE
fresh crusty bread

SERVES 4

Using a sharp knife, cut the tomatoes into thick wedges and place in a large serving dish. Drain the mozzarella cheese and roughly tear into pieces. Cut the avocados in half and remove the stones. Cut the flesh into slices, then arrange the mozzarella cheese and avocado with the tomatoes.

Mix the oil, vinegar and mustard together in a small bowl, add salt and pepper to taste, then drizzle over the salad.

Scatter the basil and olives over the top and serve immediately with fresh crusty bread.

The bulgar wheat in this salad soaks up the flavours of the other ingredients perfectly.

tabbouleh

175 g/6 oz bulgar wheat
3 tbsp extra-virgin olive oil
4 tbsp lemon juice
salt and pepper
4 spring onions
1 green pepper,
deseeded and sliced
4 tomatoes, chopped
2 tbsp chopped fresh parsley
2 tbsp chopped fresh mint
8 black olives, stoned

TO SERVE
fresh mint sprigs

SERVES 4

Place the bulgar wheat in a large bowl and add enough cold water to cover. Leave to stand for 30 minutes, or until the wheat has doubled in size. Drain well and press out as much liquid as possible. Spread out the wheat on kitchen paper to dry.

Place the wheat in a serving bowl. Mix the olive oil and lemon juice together in a jug and season to taste with salt and pepper. Pour the lemon mixture over the wheat and leave to marinate for 1 hour.

Using a sharp knife, finely chop the spring onions, then add to the salad with the green pepper, tomatoes, parsley and mint and toss lightly to mix. Top the salad with the olives and garnish with fresh mint sprigs, then serve.

This classic salad is given a modern twist with an aromatic coriander dressing.

feta cheese salad

50 g/1³/₄ oz fresh
green salad leaves
handful of fresh coriander leaves
¹/₂ cucumber, chopped
4 spring onions, finely diced
4 tomatoes, sliced
12 black olives,
stoned and sliced
140 g/5 oz feta cheese

CORIANDER DRESSING
4 tbsp extra-virgin olive oil
1 tbsp lime juice
1 tbsp chopped fresh coriander
salt and pepper

SERVES 4

Wash and drain the salad leaves, if necessary. Shred the leaves and arrange in the bottom of a large salad bowl. Add the coriander leaves, cucumber, spring onions, tomatoes and olives.

Cut the cheese into thin slices or small chunks, then transfer to the salad bowl. Mix together gently.

Put the dressing ingredients into a screw-top jar, screw on the lid tightly and shake well until thoroughly combined. Drizzle the dressing over the salad and serve immediately.

Crisp lettuce is combined with tasty pears, cheese and walnuts in this appealing salad.

orecchiette salad with pears and stilton

250 g/9 oz dried orecchiette
1 head of radicchio,
torn into pieces
1 oakleaf lettuce,
torn into pieces
2 pears
3 tbsp lemon juice
250 g/9 oz Stilton cheese, diced
55 g/2 oz chopped walnuts
4 tomatoes, quartered
1 red onion, sliced
1 carrot, grated
8 fresh basil leaves
55 g/2 oz lamb's lettuce
4 tbsp olive oil
3 tbsp white wine vinegar
salt and pepper

SERVES 4

Bring a large, heavy-based saucepan of lightly salted water to the boil. Add the pasta, return to the boil and cook for 8–10 minutes, or until tender but still firm to the bite. Drain, refresh in a bowl of cold water and drain again.

Place the radicchio and oakleaf lettuce leaves in a salad bowl. Halve the pears, remove the cores and dice the flesh. Toss the diced pear with 1 tablespoon of lemon juice in a small bowl to prevent discoloration. Top the salad with the Stilton, walnuts, pears, pasta, tomatoes, onion slices and grated carrot. Add the basil and lamb's lettuce.

Mix the remaining lemon juice and the olive oil and vinegar together in a jug, then season to taste with salt and pepper. Pour the dressing over the salad, toss and serve.

A perennial favourite, garlic bread is perfect with a range of barbecue meals.

garlic bread

150 g/5¹/₂ oz butter, softened
3 cloves garlic, crushed
2 tbsp chopped,
fresh parsley
pepper
1 large or 2 small sticks of
French bread

SERVES 6

Mix together the butter, garlic and parsley in a bowl until well combined. Season with pepper to taste and mix well.

Cut the French bread into thick slices.

Spread the flavoured butter over one side of each slice and reassemble the loaf on a large sheet of thick kitchen foil.

Wrap the bread well and barbecue over hot coals for 10–15 minutes until the butter melts and the bread is piping hot.

Serve as an accompaniment to a wide range of dishes.

 Always popular, home-made coleslaw tastes far superior to the shop-bought version.

coleslaw

225 g/8 oz white cabbage, cored and grated
225 g/8 oz carrots, peeled and grated
25 g/1 oz sugar
3 tbsp cider vinegar
salt and pepper
5 tbsp double cream, lightly whipped
2 pickled green or red peppers, drained and thinly sliced (optional)
4 tbsp finely chopped fresh parsley

SERVES 4–6

Combine the cabbage, carrots, sugar, vinegar, a large pinch of salt and pepper to taste in a large bowl, tossing the ingredients together. Cover and leave to chill for 1 hour.

Add the whipped cream and pickled peppers, if using, to the chilled vegetables and mix well. Taste and add extra sugar, vinegar or salt, if desired. Sprinkle over the parsley and serve at once. Alternatively, cover and chill until required.

This colourful salsa is packed with delicious flavours and is easy to make.

tangy tomato salsa

3 large, ripe tomatoes
$^1/_2$ red onion, finely chopped
1 large fresh green chilli, such
as jalapeño, deseeded and
finely chopped
2 tbsp chopped fresh coriander
juice of 1 lime, or to taste
salt and pepper

SERVES 4–6

Halve the tomatoes, scoop out and discard the seeds and dice the flesh. Place the flesh in a large, non-metallic bowl.

Add the onion, chilli, chopped coriander and lime juice. Season to taste with salt and pepper and stir gently to combine.

Cover and leave to chill in the refrigerator for at least 30 minutes to allow the flavours to develop before serving.

This tangy dip is full of vibrant, summery flavours, perfect for alfresco eating.

guacamole

4 avocados
2 garlic cloves
4 spring onions
3 fresh red chillies, deseeded
2 red peppers, deseeded
5 tbsp olive oil
juice of 1 1/2 limes
salt

TO GARNISH
chopped fresh coriander leaves

TO SERVE
tortilla chips

SERVES 8

Cut the avocados in half lengthways and twist the halves to separate. Remove and discard the stones and scoop out the flesh into a large bowl with a spoon. Roughly mash with a fork.

Finely chop the garlic, spring onions, chillies and peppers, then stir them into the mashed avocado. Add 4 tablespoons of the oil and the lime juice, season to taste with salt and stir well to mix. Or, if you prefer a smoother dip, process all the ingredients together in a food processor.

Transfer the guacamole to a serving bowl. Drizzle the remaining oil over the top, sprinkle with the coriander and serve with tortilla chips.

treats and tipples

Barbecued desserts make a delightful finale to any barbecue party and will be welcomed by both adults and children. Most of the recipes in this chapter are based on fruit so they can even be enjoyed by those watching their waistlines. Also featured is a selection of thirst-quenching summer drinks to refresh and delight your guests.

These warm, lightly barbecued fruit kebabs are served with a delicious chocolate dipping sauce.

fruity skewers with chocolate dip

selection of fruit – choose from oranges, bananas, strawberries, pineapple chunks, apricots, dessert apples, pears, kiwi fruit
1 tbsp lemon juice
4 tbsp clear honey
grated rind and juice of $^1/_2$ orange

CHOCOLATE SAUCE
50 g/1$^3/_4$ oz butter
50 g/1$^3/_4$ oz plain chocolate, broken into small cubes
$^1/_2$ tbsp cocoa powder
2 tbsp golden syrup

SERVES 4

Preheat the barbecue. To make the chocolate sauce, place the butter, chocolate, cocoa powder and golden syrup in a small saucepan. Heat gently on a hob or at the side of the barbecue, stirring constantly, until all of the ingredients have melted and are well combined.

To prepare the fruit, peel and core as necessary, then cut into large, bite-sized pieces or wedges as appropriate. Dip apples, pears and bananas in lemon juice to prevent discoloration. Thread the pieces of fruit on to several metal skewers.

Mix the honey, orange juice and rind together. Heat gently if required and brush over the fruit.

Cook the fruit skewers over warm coals for 5–10 minutes, until hot, brushing on more glaze. Serve with the chocolate sauce.

 Foil-wrapped apples bake to perfection on the barbecue and are a delightful finale to any meal.

barbecued baked apples

4 medium cooking apples
25 g/1 oz walnuts, chopped
25 g/1 oz ground almonds
25 g/1 oz light
muscovado sugar
25 g/1 oz glazed
cherries, chopped
25 g/1 oz stem ginger, chopped
1 tbsp Amaretto (optional)
50 g/1³/₄ oz butter

TO SERVE
single cream

SERVES 4

Preheat the barbecue. Core the apples and using a knife, score each one around the centre to prevent the apple skins splitting during barbecuing.

To make the filling, mix the walnuts, almonds, sugar, cherries, ginger and Amaretto, if using, together in a small bowl. Spoon the filling mixture into each apple, pushing it down into the hollowed-out core. Mound a little of the filling mixture on top of each apple.

Place each apple on a large square of double thickness foil and generously dot all over with the butter. Wrap up the foil so that the apple is completely enclosed.

Cook the foil parcels over hot coals for 25–30 minutes, or until tender. Transfer the apples to warmed serving plates and serve with cream.

 Bananas are very sweet when barbecued, and conveniently come in their own protective wrapping.

chocolate rum bananas

1 tbsp butter, softened
225 g/8 oz plain or milk chocolate
4 large bananas
2 tbsp rum

TO SERVE
crème fraîche, mascarpone cheese or ice cream
grated nutmeg

SERVES 4

Take four 25-cm/10-inch squares of aluminium foil and brush them with butter.

Cut the chocolate into very small pieces. Make a careful slit lengthways in the peel of each banana, and open just wide enough to insert the chocolate. Place the chocolate pieces inside the bananas, along their lengths, then close them up.

Wrap each stuffed banana in a square of foil, then barbecue them over hot coals for about 5–10 minutes, or until the chocolate has melted inside the bananas. Remove from the barbecue, place the bananas on individual serving plates and pour some rum into each banana.

Serve at once with crème fraîche, mascarpone cheese or ice cream, topped with nutmeg.

Fresh, succulent pineapple and rum are a magical combination.

totally tropical pineapple

1 pineapple
3 tbsp dark rum
2 tbsp muscovado sugar
1 tsp ground ginger
4 tbsp unsalted butter, melted

SERVES 4

Preheat the barbecue. Using a sharp knife, cut off the crown of the pineapple, then cut the fruit into 2-cm/¾-inch thick slices. Cut away the peel from each slice and flick out the 'eyes' with the point of the knife. Stamp out the cores with an apple corer or small pastry cutter.

Mix the rum, sugar, ginger and butter together in a jug, stirring constantly, until the sugar has dissolved. Brush the pineapple rings with the rum mixture.

Cook the pineapple rings over hot coals for 3–4 minutes on each side. Transfer to serving plates and serve immediately with the remaining rum mixture poured over them.

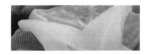

Delicious pieces of exotic fruit are cooked in a sweetly scented sauce.

exotic fruity parcels

1 papaya
1 mango
1 star fruit
1 tbsp grenadine
3 tbsp orange juice

TO SERVE
single cream or
natural yogurt

SERVES 4

Cut the papaya in half, scoop out the seeds and discard them. Peel the papaya and cut the flesh into thick slices.

Prepare the mango by cutting it lengthwise in half either side of the central stone. Score each mango half in a criss-cross pattern. Push each mango half inside out to separate the cubes and cut them away from the peel.

Using a sharp knife, thickly slice the star fruit. Place all of the fruit in a bowl and mix them together.

Mix the grenadine and orange juice together and pour over the fruit. Leave to marinate for at least 30 minutes.

Divide the fruit among 4 double thickness squares of kitchen foil and gather up the edges to form a parcel that encloses the fruit. Place the foil parcels on a rack set over warm coals and barbecue the fruit for 15–20 minutes.

Serve the fruit in the parcel, with single cream or yogurt offered separately.

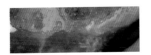

This rich, fruity dessert makes an indulgent end to a special occasion barbecue party.

special peach melba

2 large peaches, peeled, halved and stoned
1 tbsp light brown sugar
1 tbsp Amaretto liqueur
450 g/1 lb fresh raspberries, plus extra to decorate
115 g/4 oz icing sugar
600 ml/1 pint vanilla ice cream

SERVES 4

Place the peach halves in a large, shallow dish and sprinkle with the brown sugar. Pour the Amaretto liqueur over them, cover with clingfilm and leave to marinate for 1 hour.

Meanwhile, using the back of a spoon, press the raspberries through a fine sieve set over a bowl. Discard the contents of the sieve. Stir the icing sugar into the raspberry purée. Cover the bowl with clingfilm and leave to chill in the refrigerator until required.

Preheat the barbecue. Drain the peach halves, reserving the marinade. Cook over hot coals, turning and brushing frequently with the reserved marinade, for 3–5 minutes. To serve, put 2 scoops of vanilla ice cream in each of 4 sundae glasses, top with a peach half and spoon the raspberry sauce over it. Decorate with whole raspberries and serve.

Citrus flavours turn this into an irresistible drink.

iced citrus tea

300 ml/10 fl oz water
2 tea bags
100 ml/3¹/₂ fl oz orange juice
4 tbsp lime juice
1–2 tbsp brown sugar

TO SERVE
wedge of lime
granulated sugar
8 ice cubes
slices of orange, lemon or lime

SERVES 2

Pour the water into a saucepan and bring to the boil. Remove from the heat, add the tea bags and leave to infuse for 5 minutes. Remove the tea bags and then leave the tea to cool to room temperature (about 30 minutes). Transfer to a jug, cover with clingfilm and chill in the refrigerator for at least 45 minutes.

When the tea has chilled, pour in the orange juice and lime juice. Add sugar to taste.

Take two glasses and rub the rims with a wedge of lime, then dip them in granulated sugar to frost. Put the ice cubes into the glasses and pour over the tea. Decorate the rims with slices of fresh orange, lemon or lime and serve.

This classic cooler is a well-loved, traditional favourite.

home-made **lemonade**

150 ml/5 fl oz water
6 tbsp sugar
1 tsp grated lemon rind
125 ml/4 fl oz lemon juice

TO SERVE
lemon wedges
granulated sugar
6 ice cubes
sparkling water
slices of lemon

SERVES 2

Put the water, sugar and grated lemon rind into a small saucepan and bring to the boil, stirring constantly. Continue to boil, stirring, for 5 minutes.

Remove from the heat and leave to cool to room temperature. Stir in the lemon juice, then transfer to a jug, cover with clingfilm and chill in the refrigerator for at least 2 hours.

When the lemonade has almost finished chilling, take two glasses and rub the rims with a wedge of lemon, then dip them in granulated sugar to frost. Put the ice cubes into the glasses.

Remove the lemon syrup from the refrigerator, pour it over the ice and top up with sparkling water. The ratio should be one part lemon syrup to three parts sparkling water. Stir well to mix, decorate with slices of fresh lemon and serve.

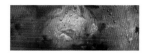

This favourite drink is an ideal refresher on a hot summer's afternoon.

pimm's no. 1

ice
1 measure Pimm's no. 1
lemonade

TO SERVE
strips of cucumber peel
sprigs of fresh mint
slices of orange and lemon

SERVES 1

Fill a chilled large glass two-thirds full with ice and pour in the Pimm's.

Top up with lemonade and stir gently.

Dress with a twist of cucumber peel, a sprig of fresh mint and a slice of orange and lemon.

A perfect long drink for a crowd of friends or family at a summer barbecue.

sangria

juice of 1 orange
juice of 1 lemon
2 tbsp caster sugar
ice
1 orange, thinly sliced
1 lemon, thinly sliced
1 bottle red wine, chilled
lemonade

SERVES 6

Stir orange and lemon juice with the sugar in a large bowl or jug.

When the sugar has dissolved, add few cubes ice, sliced fruit and wine.

Leave to chill for 1 hour, if possible, to allow the flavours to develop. Add the lemonade and more ice to taste and serve.

INDEX